BLAZERS

STRANGE *but* TRUE SCIENCE

BY STACY B. DAVIDS

Reading Consultant:
Barbara J. Fox
Reading Specialist
North Carolina State University

CAPSTONE PRESS
a capstone imprint

Blazers is published by Capstone Press,
151 Good Counsel Drive, P.O. Box 669, Mankato, Minnesota 56002.
www.capstonepub.com

Books published by Capstone Press are manufactured with paper
containing at least 10 percent post-consumer waste.

Library of Congress Cataloging-in-Publication Data
Davids, Stacy B.
  Strange but true science / by Stacy B. Davids.
     p. cm.— (Blazers. Strange but true)
  Summary: "Describes unusual science experiments and breakthrough medical procedures"
—Provided by publisher.
  Includes bibliographical references and index.
  ISBN 978-1-4296-4552-2 (library binding)
  1. Science—Experiments—Juvenile literature. 2. Science—Miscellanea—Juvenile literature.
  I. Title. II. Series.
  Q182.3.D38 2011
  500—dc22   2010003660

Editorial Credits
Editor: Kathryn Clay
Designer: Kyle Grenz
Media Researcher: Svetlana Zhurkin
Production Specialist: Laura Manthe

Photo Credits
AP Images/PA, 24–25; Yonhap/Choi Byung-kil, 4–5
Audubon Nature Institute/Anahid Pahhlawanian, 8–9
Getty Images/Brandi Simons, 28–29; Joe Raedle, 11 (inset); Matt Cardy, 26–27; PPL
      Therapeutics via BWP Media, 20–21
Landov/Maxppp/Frantz Bouton, 18–19
Newscom, 6–7; Splash News, 10–11; Splash News/Cleveland Clinic, 13; WENN, cover, 14–15
Photo Researchers/Pascal Goetgheluck, 16–17-
Shutterstock/Andrejs Pidjass, cover (texture); Emin Kuliyev, 22–23

TABLE OF CONTENTS

IMPORTANT SCIENCE

Cats glow in the dark. People swallow cameras. A person gets a new face. These advances in science may be strange. But each one has an important purpose.

TOE-TO-THUMB TRANSPLANT

If you ever lose your thumb, you may be able to replace it with your toe. Doctors remove the big toe. They transplant the toe where the thumb used to be.

transplant—a surgical operation in which a damaged body part is replaced by a healthy one

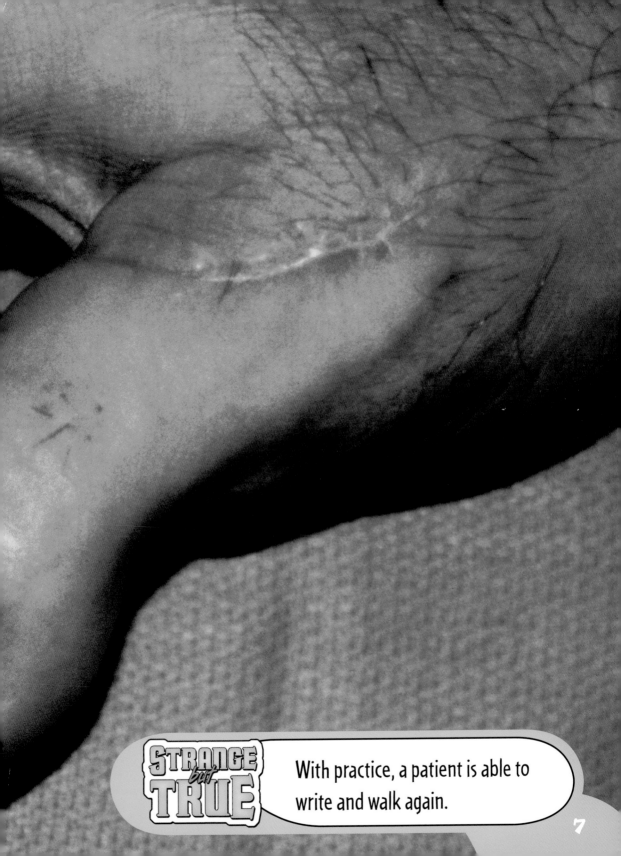

STRANGE but TRUE

With practice, a patient is able to write and walk again.

7

GLOW-IN-THE-DARK CAT

This cat looks normal in the daylight. But it glows in the dark. The cat glows because scientists added a special gene. They wanted to see if they could add a gene that was not natural to cats.

gene—one of the parts of the cells of all living things; genes are passed from parents to children

Scientists hope to add disease-fighting genes to humans one day.

EYE-TOOTH

Doctors can use teeth to help blind people see. They reshape a tooth and drill a hole in it. Then they put a lens in the tooth. The tooth holds the new eye in place.

lens—a curved part of the eye that lets in light

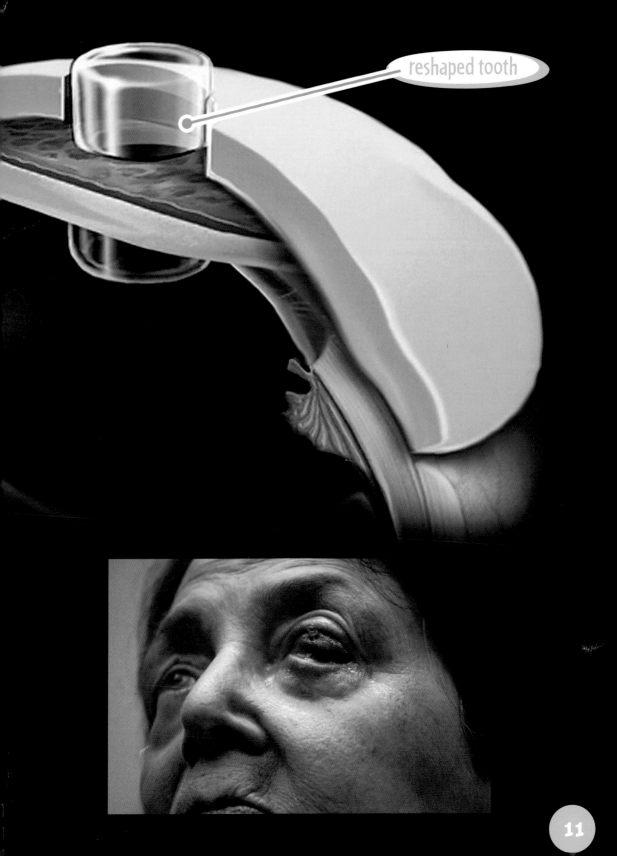

FACE TRANSPLANT

A person with a serious face injury may need a transplant. Doctors take the face from a donor. They attach the donor's skin, veins, muscle, and bone to a patient. Afterward the patient can breathe, eat, and smile.

donor—someone who agrees to give his or her body to medical science to help sick or injured people

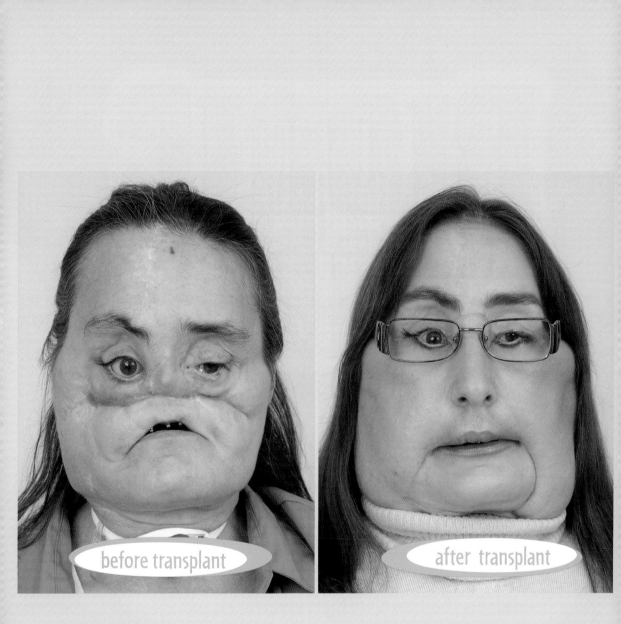

before transplant

after transplant

Because face shapes are different, the patient doesn't look like the donor.

BIONIC HAND

Bionic hands sound like something found in movies. But real people use them every day. A bionic hand attaches to electrodes on the skin. A person controls the hand with an electric signal.

bionic—to do with mechanical parts designed to replace limbs or other parts of the body

electrode—a point through which an electric current can flow into or out of a device or substance

STRANGE but TRUE

The hand's fake skin can be painted to match a person's skin color.

ROBOT SURGERY

Imagine having an operation done by a robot. Some doctors use robots during surgery. A doctor controls four robot arms at once. One arm holds a camera. The other arms cut and sew.

STRANGE but TRUE

A doctor can control the robot from 20 feet (6 meters) away.

robot

CAMERA PILLS

Need a closer look at the lunch you just ate? Doctors use tiny cameras to see inside people's intestines. Patients swallow the cameras like pills. The pictures can be seen on a computer.

intestine—one of the long, hollow tubes below the stomach

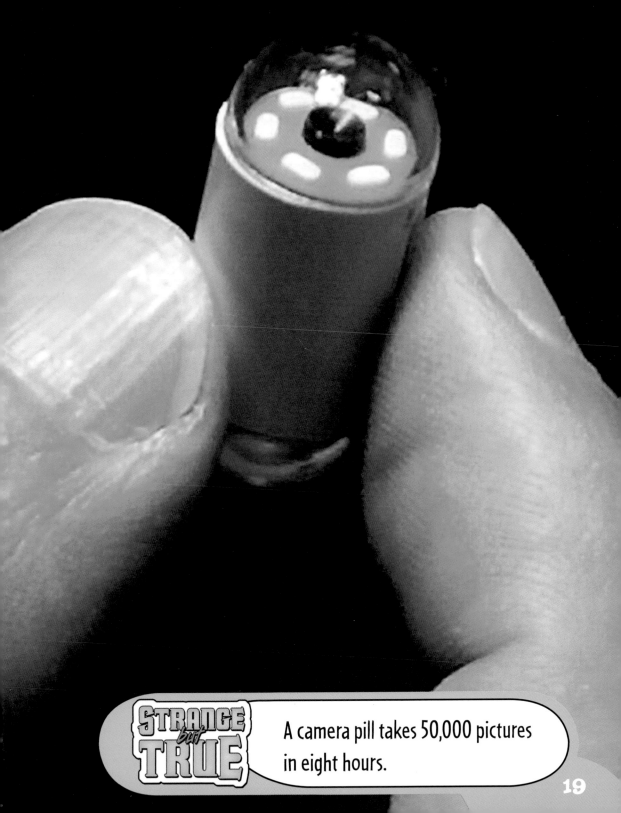

STRANGE but TRUE

A camera pill takes 50,000 pictures in eight hours.

CLONING

cloned pigs

STRANGE but TRUE

People can now clone their pets.
The cost can be up to $150,000.

Scientists use cloning to make copies of animals. They take cells from one animal to create another animal with the same DNA.

clone—to use an animal's cells to grow another identical animal

DNA—material in cells that gives people their individual characteristics

CLONING POSSIBILITIES

Scientists have talked about cloning other things. Some people want to clone dinosaurs. But doing so is unlikely because scientists don't have enough dinosaur DNA. Cloning organs is another option. Cloned livers and kidneys could replace diseased body parts.

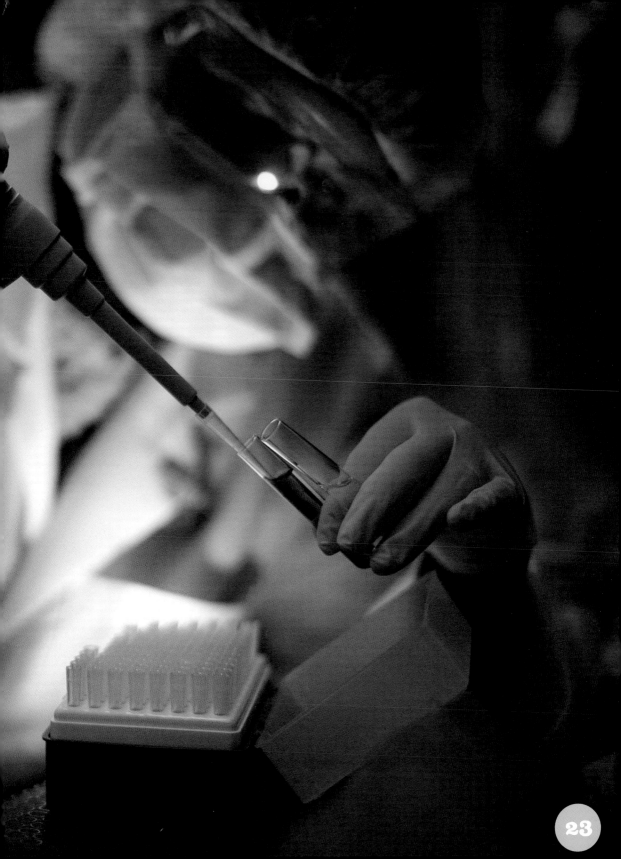

EAR MOUSE

Doctors wanted to grow body parts in a lab. They made a plastic ear mold and added cow cells. The cells needed a living thing to grow. Doctors placed the mold under a mouse's skin. The cells grew into the shape of the ear.

STRANGE *but* TRUE

Doctors hope to someday grow other body parts.

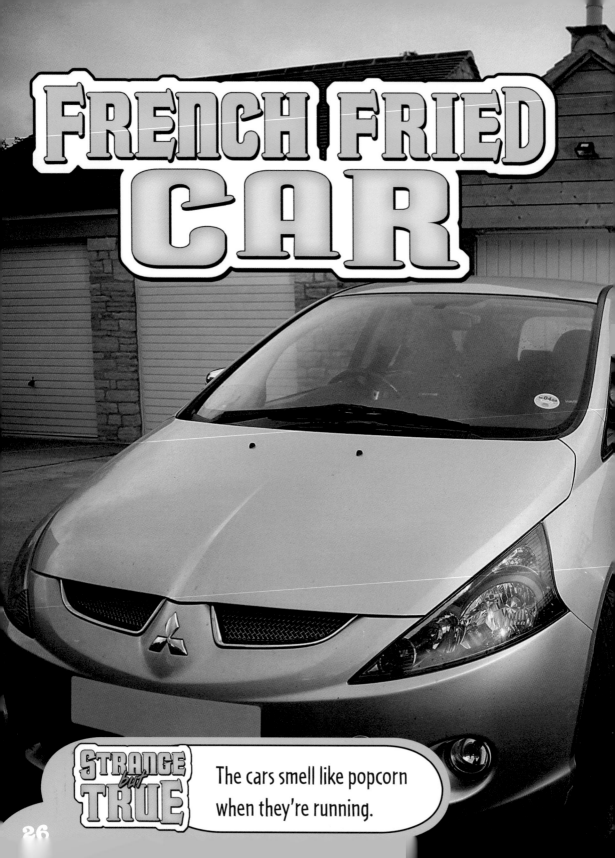

FRENCH FRIED CAR

STRANGE but TRUE

The cars smell like popcorn when they're running.

Some cars run on French fry oil.
Drivers get used vegetable oil from fast
food restaurants. Once the oil is heated,
the car's engine burns it like diesel.

diesel—a heavy fuel that burns to make power

IMPROVING LIVES

French fry cars, camera pills, and bionic hands are unusual. But strange science can improve people's lives.

GLOSSARY

bionic (bye-ON-ik)—to do with mechanical parts designed to replace limbs or other parts of the body

cell (SEL)—the smallest unit of a living thing

clone (KLOHN)—to use an animal's cells to grow another identical animal

diesel (DEE-zuhl)—a heavy fuel that burns to make power

DNA (dee-en-AY)—material in cells that gives people their individual characteristics

donor (DOH-nur)—someone who agrees to give his or her body to medical science to help sick or injured people

electrode (i-LEK-trode)—a point through which an electric current can flow into or out of a device or substance

gene (JEEN)—one of the parts of the cells of all living things; genes are passed from parents to children and determine how you look and the way you grow

intestine (in-TESS-tin)—one of the long, hollow tubes below the stomach; the intestines digest food and absorb water and nutrients

lens (LENZ)—a curved part of the eye that lets in light

transplant (TRANSS-plant)—a surgical operation in which a damaged body part is replaced by a healthy one

READ MORE

Cohen, Marina. *Genetic Engineering*. Let's Relate to Genetics. New York: Crabtree Pub., 2010.

Gray, Susan Heinrichs. *Transplants*. Innovation in Medicine. Ann Arbor, Mich.: Cherry Lake Pub., 2009.

Horn, Geoffrey M. *Biofuels*. Energy Today. New York: Chelsea Clubhouse, 2010.

INTERNET SITES

FactHound offers a safe, fun way to find Internet sites related to this book. All of the sites on FactHound have been researched by our staff.

Here's all you do:

Visit *www.facthound.com*

FactHound will fetch the best sites for you!

INDEX